Thank you for your support!

JR

Justin Robinson

BIOGRAPHY

Hey guys! I am Chef JRob, and I would like to start by thanking you for your support of Just In Time. This is my first cookbook, and it came with many trials and tribulations to form this work of art for your kitchen. I am proud to present a high quality, go-to recipe book for your daily kitchen needs. Whether it be tips and tricks, quick kitchen hacks, or delicious recipes for my early morning grinders, on the go health gurus, or romantic DIYers; all these recipes are Just In Time for you!

I'm a self-taught chef reigning from Mobile, Alabama. I received my Bachelor's degree in Biomedical Sciences from Auburn University and my Master's degree in Public Health from Mercer University. Although I'm bringing a Cajun kick to Atlanta's culinary scene, my cooking journey began my freshman year of college, on a hot plate. Friends would often stop by and taste what I had cooked up in my dorm room. I stayed in good graces with my hall director by sliding her a free meal weekly! My love for cooking has grown from those very humble beginnings, and my passion for cooking has taken me places I never would have fathomed. Cooking has placed me in front of well-known figures that I never would've imagined I would work for! Through this work, I'm excited to share some of my delicious one-of-a-kind recipes, educate you on some key healthy cooking tips, and inspire you to pursue your dreams to the fullest!

When you are living in your purpose and married to your passion, your success is limitless and your happiness will be eternal! Aside from the recipes, I want this book to be a living testimony of the greatness God has in store for you when you're obedient to His word.
I went to school to pursue an education in hopes of becoming a pharmacist. Honestly, I chose this path because my parents thought it would be a good fit. People will always have health issues, so pharmaceuticals will always be a leading industry in the US. Additionally, we all know it pays well, so it's a very stable job, to say the least. After 3 years of study, and working as a pharmacy technician, I switched my concentration my Junior year to become a Surgical Physician Assistant. When my senior year arrived, I applied to 20 schools, but I wasn't accepted to any. I had all the credentials needed to be a competitive applicant, aside from a high GPA; However, my lab partners in my science classes who had the same GPA with fewer credentials were getting accepted. So, what was wrong with me? This was the worst feeling in the world. After I crossed the best fraternity in the world and complet-

ed undergrad, my plan B and plan C for my life did not work out. I had nothing to show for 4 years of hard work. I took a gap year back at home in Mobile and retook classes to increase my GPA and working as a phlebotomist.

I was a damn good sticker if you ask me! Yeah, a college grad making $10/hr trying to figure out life. My co-workers at the hospital found out that I liked to cook, and, on my off days, I would prepare meals for them and their significant others. I did this at no cost, so of course, word of mouth spread like crazy! One weekend, a friend of mine asked if I could cook for him and his significant other, instead of them spending money at a restaurant. That was the moment it clicked for me! My buddy, Richard Lucas, was my first paid booking ever. I prepared a 3-course meal for them, at my parent's house, and I was so grateful for the $50 made. Then it clicked even more. I thought to myself, Wow, it took me 3 hours to cook this and I made $50 (5 hours of work at the hospital), and I was able to make a lasting memory for them. A year later, I moved to Atlanta for grad school. Once again, I was trying to increase my GPA and become a more competitive applicant. Instead of transferring hospitals, I decided I would cook to make money so I could solely focus on my studies because I needed every A I could get. I was still battling with self-doubt, thinking I wasn't smart enough to be a PA, all while trying to make a name for myself and build my own legacy. After 2 years of grad school, I grew my business, and more importantly, my confidence. I had celebrity clientele, became consistently busy on the weekends, made the top 80 of MasterChef, participated in the Iron Chef Showdown, graduated with a 3.9 GPA, received the 1st year Most Outstanding Student Award and Dean's Excellence Award my 2nd year, and produced my first scientific publication. I proudly list these accomplishments JUST TO SAY, don't ever doubt your capabilities; don't ever think you're not going to be successful; don't ever count yourself out! It's okay not to have everything aligned because God's path for you is never clear. You must take every step in His direction. I completed graduate school with the competitive GPA needed to get accepted into PA school, acquired triple the number of patient care hours needed, and earned honors and awards that were more appealing to an acceptance board. Even still, I remember praying and asking God what my next step in life would be—to reapply to PA school or dive fully into my culinary business? The day I graduated with my Masters in Public Health, my parents asked at the dinner table, "When are you going to apply for PA school, and which schools are you looking at?" I took a deep breath and replied, "I'm going to run Chef JRob full time."

From Mobile, to my dorm room, to Atlanta the one thing that never wavered was my passion for cooking. Don't be afraid to connect deeper and discover your purpose in life. Find what you are placed on Earth to do. Yes, income may not be as "steady" as you would like, and yes there are other things that appear would be a "safer" route. However, if you can honestly, go to sleep at night loving what you're doing, your dreams will inspire the next person's reality.

My Mentality: You don't have to be the smartest or most talented person in the room, but you must be the most hard-working person in the room. That's what it takes to be great. That's why I call myself Atlanta's Greatest Chef. Now… Let's let the good times roll!

CONTENT

SPICY - SWEET - SALTY - SOUR - UMAMI

INTRODUCTION	06
JUICES, SMOOTHIES, & BOWLS	10
VEGAN, VEGETARIAN, & SALADS	18
BOTTOMLESS BRUNCH	38
SOUTHERN HOSPITALITY	56
BREAKING BREAD	70
SURF & TURF	96

JUST IN TIME

Justin Robinson

Master Chef
Justin Robinson
The Chef JRob Experience

Creative Director
Tianna "Gabby" Clark
Senior Designer
Eccentric Outcasts LLC.

Photographer
Joshua "Danny" Garrett
Senior Photographer
351 Productions

Publisher
Evan Dean
Dominic Ligon
Senior Editors
Flash Publishing and Media LLC.

©2020 Justin Robinson. All rights reserved.

COOKBOOK

CUTTING TIME IN THE KITCHEN

the
introduction

Justin Robinson

USING ALL 5 SENSES

A B O U T
THE COOKBOOK

Fire up the stove! No matter your experience in the kitchen, *"Just In Time"* is your culinary tool to enhance your flavor profile, fine tune your technique, and introduce your palate to some out-of-this-world flavors! The array of recipes will cover your breakfast, lunch, dinner, and mid-day snack cravings!

Please when you recreate these recipes tag my social media @chef.jrob with hashtag #JustInTime so that we can further connect! Let's Rock N'Roll!

My Purpose

CHANGING LIVES ONE TASTEBUD AT A TIME

With the layouts in this cook book, each ingredient is linked to the amount for the recipe. Each step is broken down and numbered for an easy process.

Justin Robinson

Herb fla

ROSEMARY:
AN AROMATIC TOUCH TO ELEVATE GRILLED MEATS, POTATOES, AND COCKTAILS. PAIRS WELL WITH BERRIES. THE NOTES ON THE PALATE SHOULD BE PINEY, ALMOST LIKE A CHARRED WOOD..

SAGE:
AN EXCEPTIONAL FRESH HERB THAT ENHANCES THE FLAVOR IN CHICKPEAS OR SAUCES. BOLD IN FLAVOR WITH A PEPPERY/MINTY AFTER BITE.

PARSLEY:
THE ULTIMATE GARNISHER. GRASSY AND BITTER IN FLAVOR. PARSLEY CAN BE FOUND AS A FLAT-LEAF (ITALIAN) OR CURLY IN APPEARANCE.

THYME:
AN ALL-PURPOSE HERB THAT SHINES UNDER A HOT BUTTER BASE AND SHINES AS A FRESH GARNISH WITH A SQUEEZE OF LEMON. THE NOTES ON THE PALATE SHOULD BE REFRESHING, MINTY, AND POSSIBLY WOODY WHEN BASED WITH BUTTER.

or Profiles

MINT:
A VERSATILE HERB WITH A RECOGNIZABLE FLVOR. PERFECT FOR LAMB, MOJITOS, AND GOES HAND IN HAND WITH LIME.

CHIVES:
A GREAT ALTERNATIVE GARNISH WITH DELICATE NOTES OF ONION ON THE PALATE.

BASIL:
AN AROMATIC ROBUST HERB THAT IS THE STAR IN PESTO AND MARINARA SAUCES. GREAT FOR GARNISHING PASTA DISHES.

DILL:
SEAFOOD'S BEST FRIEND ADDS A PUNGENT PICKLE FLAVOR TO THE PROTEIN OR STOCK.

JUICES, SMOO

KALE TONIC JUICE

|  SERVING 1 PERSON | PREP 3 MINUTES |  COOK 2 MINUTES |  TOTAL 5 MINUTES |

FORMULA

INGREDIENTS	AMOUNT
PEELED LEMON	½
PEELED LIME	½
KALE	1 BUNCH
MINERAL WATER	2 ¼ CUPS
GINGER	SNAP
HONEY	4 TBSP

PROCESS

1. After mixture is well blended, remove juice from blender and pour through a sieve to remove excess pulp. Ingredients can be placed in blender or juicer.

MORNING RISE JUICE

| SERVING 1 PERSON | PREP 3 MINUTES |  COOK 5 MINUTES |  TOTAL 8 MINUTES |

FORMULA

INGREDIENTS	AMOUNT
CARROTS	3
PEACH	1
MANGO	1

PROCESS

1. Cut and remove the seed from the peach and remove the skin from the mango before adding ingredients into the juicer.

STRAWBERRY BANANA MANGO SMOOTHIE

SERVING	PREP	COOK	TOTAL
2 PERSONS	3 MINUTES	5 MINUTES	8 MINUTES

FORMULA

INGREDIENTS	AMOUNT
FROZEN STRAWBERRIES	7
FROZEN MANGO	1/2
FROZEN BANANA	1
VANILLA	1 TSP
GREEK YOGURT	2 TBSP

PROCESS

1. Combine all ingredients into a blender. Blend ingredients on a low speed while gradually increasing to a higher speed until smoothly blended.

COFFEE BEAN SMOOTHIE

SERVING	PREP	COOK	TOTAL
6-8 PERSONS	3 MINUTES	5 MINUTES	8 MINUTES

FORMULA

INGREDIENTS	AMOUNT
COFFEE	1 CUP
ICE	4 CUPS
VANILLA CHAI	¾ CUP
HONEY	2 TBSP

PROCESS

1. Combine all ingredients into a blender. Blend ingredients on a low speed while gradually increasing to a higher speed until smoothly blended.

PIÑA COLADA SMOOTHIE

 **SERVING** 6–8 PERSONS  **PREP** 3 MINUTES  **COOK** 5 MINUTES  **TOTAL** 8 MINUTES

FORMULA

INGREDIENTS	AMOUNT
BANANA	1
FRESHLY CUT PINEAPPLE	2 CUPS
PINEAPPLE JUICE	¾ CUPS
COCONUT MILK	¾ CUPS
ICE	4 CUPS
VANILLA EXTRACT	1 TSP

PROCESS

1. Combine all ingredients into a blender. Blend ingredients on a low speed while gradually increasing to a higher speed until smoothly blended.

DEEP BLUE SEA BOWL

SERVING	PREP	COOK	TOTAL
1 PERSON	5 MINUTES	10 MINUTES	15 MINUTES

FORMULA

INGREDIENTS	AMOUNT
FROZEN BLACKBERRIES	½ CUP
FROZEN STRAWBERRIES	½ CUP
FROZEN BLUEBERRIES	1 CUP
FROZEN RASPBERRIES	1 CUP
BANANAS	1
VANILLA CHAI	2 CUPS
HONEY	2 TBSP

PROCESS

I. Combine all ingredients into a blender. Blend on a low speed while gradually increasing to a higher speed until smoothly blended. The thicker the better!

II. Blue Spirulina Superfood powder blend was used to achieve the deep blue sea coloration.

ACAI BERRY BOWL

SERVING	**PREP**	**COOK**	**TOTAL**
1 PERSON	5 MINUTES	10 MINUTES	15 MINUTES

FORMULA

INGREDIENTS	AMOUNT
WATER	1 CUP
PACK OF ACAI BERRY	3 ½ OZ
FROZEN BLUEBERRIES	½ CUP
FROZEN BLACKBERRIES	½ CUP
FROZEN STRAWBERRIES	7
FROZEN RASPBERRIES	½ CUP
FROZEN BANANA	1

PROCESS

1. Combine all ingredients into a blender. Blend on a low speed while gradually increasing to a higher speed until smoothly blended. The thicker the better!

PEACH MANGO MATCHA BOWL

 SERVING 1 PERSON   **PREP** 3 MINUTES   **COOK** 5 MINUTES   **TOTAL** 8 MINUTES

FORMULA

INGREDIENTS	AMOUNT
FROZEN MANGOS	2
FROZEN PEACH	1
FROZEN KIWI	1
VANILLA CHAI	1/2 CUP

PROCESS

Combine all ingredients into a blender. Blend on a low speed while gradually increasing to a higher speed until smoothly blended. Matcha Superfood powder blend was used to achieve coloration.

TROPICAL PASSION BOWL

 **SERVING** 1 PERSON   **PREP** 3 MINUTES   **COOK** 5 MINUTES    **TOTAL** 8 MINUTES

FORMULA

INGREDIENTS	AMOUNT
FROZEN MANGO	1 CUP
FROZEN RASPBERRIES	½ CUP
VANILLA CHAI	½ CUP

PROCESS

I. Combine all ingredients into a blender. Blend on a low speed while gradually increasing to a higher speed until smoothly blended. The thicker the better!

II. Tropical Superfood was used to achieve color.

JUICES, SMOOTHIES, & BOWLS

TARIAN, & SALADS

VEGAN
COCONUT CURRY CHICKPEAS
IN PINEAPPLE BOWL

SERVING
4-5 PERSONS

PREP
7 MINUTES

COOK
25 MINUTES

TOTAL
32 MINUTES

FORMULA

INGREDIENTS	AMOUNT
CHICKPEAS	1 CAN
COCONUT MILK	13.5 OZ
CILANTRO	½ BUNCH
WHITE GRAIN RICE	2 CUPS
TOMATO PASTE	2 TBSP
ONION	1
PINEAPPLE	1
CURRY POWDER	2 TBSP
SALT	5 TBSP
PEPPER	3 TBSP
CAJUN SEASONING	½ TBSP
MEDITERRANEAN SEASONING	1 TBSP
WATER	3 CUPS
CANOLA OIL	¼ CUP
SAGE LEAVES	4 LEAVES
BUTTER	1 TBSP
LIME	1

PINEAPPLE
HOLLOWING OUT FOR PLATING

I. Cut pineapple in half from the stem to the base (including the leaf stem).
II. Hollow out pineapple by cutting a rectangular box in the center of each half.
III. Slice that box into 4 pieces horizontally and vertically for easy extraction.
IV. Take a spoon and carve out each cube of pineapple.
V. Plate your rice on one half of the pineapple, and curry chickpeas on another half. Take a bite and enjoy!

PROCESS

CHICKPEAS
I. Boil 3 cups of water in a pot.
II. Strain the canned fluid off your chickpeas and add them into the boiling water.
III. Cook for 5-7 minutes, or until the outer casing of the chickpeas start to come off.
IV. Strain chickpeas from water and place them aside. Add ¼ cup of canola oil into the dry pot.
V. Chop up 4 leaves of fresh sage, and add in chickpeas.
VI. Lightly sauté for 2 minutes with ½ tablespoon of salt, ½ tablespoon of pepper, and 1 tablespoon of Mediterranean seasoning on medium-high heat.
VII. Combine chickpeas with curry sauce.

CURRY
THE KEY IS TO WORK SMARTER NOT HARDER!
I. Add your coconut milk to a saucepan and allow it to simmer on medium heat for 6 minutes, or until it starts to bubble.
II. Reduce the heat to medium-low, and add 2 tablespoons of tomato paste, 2 tablespoons curry powder, and ½ tablespoon of each of the following: pepper, salt, and Cajun seasoning. Give it some wrist work and cook for 5 minutes.
III. On medium-low heat, combine chickpeas with curry mixture and stir until mixture thickens.

FLAVOR UP YOUR RICE!
CILANTRO LIME
I. Use a 2:1 ratio (2 cups of water per 1 cup of rice).
II. Boil rice over medium-high, and add a squeeze of 1 lime and ½ bunch of chopped fresh cilantro. Stir occasionally every 5 to 6 minutes.
III. Season rice with 4 tablespoons of salt and 2 tablespoons of pepper once water is fully absorbed.
IV. Toss in 1 tablespoon of butter and stir!

V E G A N

RASPBERRY CHIPOTLE JACKFRUIT

SERVING	PREP	COOK	TOTAL
6-8 PERSONS	5 MINUTES	30 MINUTES	35 MINUTES

FORMULA

INGREDIENTS	AMOUNT
JACKFRUIT	2 CANS
RASPBERRIES	PLATING
BUTTER LEAF LETTUCE	1 HEAD
RASPBERRY CHIPOTLE	1 TBSP
PEPPER	½ TBSP
CANOLA OIL	1 CUP
LIME	½ LIME
HONEY	2 TBSP
PARSLEY	1 TBSP
SWEET PEPPERS	5

PROCESS

JACKFRUIT

I. Take the jackfruit out of the can and slice it until it appears like shredded chicken.
II. Drizzle two tablespoons of honey over your jackfruit (full 4 second count - squeeze)
III. Combine in a bowl: 1 tablespoon of raspberry chipotle seasoning, ½ tablespoon of salt and pepper each, and 1 tablespoon of parsley. Mix in honey glazed jackfruit.
IV. Sauté in a cast iron skillet on high heat for 4 minutes while mixing thoroughly.
V. Add ¼ cup of canola oil and a squeeze of ½ lime to enhance flavor.
VI. Mix throughout the skillet. Cover and simmer over medium heat for 10 minutes.
VII. As the jackfruit cooks for approximately 3 minutes, it will absorb the oil; you will need to replenish it with ¼ cup of oil and continue to mix throughout the cast iron skillet. Recover.

VIII. Mince 4-5 mini sweet peppers to add a refreshing taste!
IX. Add sweet peppers to your jackfruit, and cook for an additional 10 minutes with ¼ cup of canola oil.
X. At the 10 minute mark, you'll see a nice char on your jackfruit. That is exactly what you want! The jackfruit should resemble pulled pork.
XI. Add ¼ cup of oil, and cook at medium heat for another 5 minutes, while mixing it every 2 minutes.
XII. Plate jackfruit inside of the butter leaf lettuce and enjoy!

Tip: If Chipotle Raspberry has too much of a kick...add more honey to reduce the amount of back kick.

Justin Robinson

VVS | VEGAN, VEGETARIAN, & SALADS

VEGETARIAN

STUFFED PORTOBELLO MUSHROOM

SERVING	PREP	COOK	TOTAL
2 PERSONS	3 MINUTES	20 MINUTES	23 MINUTES

FORMULA

INGREDIENTS	AMOUNT
PORTOBELLO MUSHROOMS	2
CHERRY TOMATOES	6
MOZZARELLA CHUNKS	1 PACK
BALSAMIC GLAZE	1 BOTTLE
SEA SALT	1 CUP
PEPPER	1 TBSP
BUTTER	1 TBSP
BASIL	3 LEAVES
GARLIC	1 CLOVE
TARRAGON	7 LEAVES

PROCESS

GARLIC-TARRAGON HOUSE BUTTER
SCRATCH THE STORE, MAKE IT YOURSELF!

I. Mix 1 clove of minced garlic, a pinch of minced tarragon, and 2 tablespoons of butter together!

MUSHROOMS

I. Use a small spoon to run across the outside of the Portobello mushrooms until gills are removed.
II. Cut the little stub off the stem.
III. Ground up ½ tablespoon of salt & pepper per mushroom covering the entire surface.
IV. Pop it in the oven at 385°F for 5 minutes to dry out any of the gills that may have been overlooked.
V. Remove the mushrooms from the oven and lightly rub a garlic-tarragon house butter over the top and the inside of the mushroom.
VI. Add mozzarella chunks and fresh cherry tomatoes to your mushroom.
VII. Place into the oven at 385 °F for an additional 10 minutes, and then broil for 5 minutes until cheese and tomatoes achieve a nice crisp skin.
VIII. While your mushrooms are cooking away in the oven, take some basil leaves and roll them into a cylinder formation. Make nice fine cuts for elegance. This will be an aromatic garnish for your stuffed mushrooms.

Tip: For the best results use deep mushrooms.

VVS | VEGAN, VEGETARIAN, & SALADS

SALADS

MIXED BERRY CHICKEN SALAD

SERVING
2 PERSONS

PREP
3 MINUTES

COOK
12 MINUTES

TOTAL
15 MINUTES

FORMULA

INGREDIENTS	AMOUNT
SPRING MIX	1 BAG
RADISHES	2
AVOCADOS	2
CHICKEN BREAST	1
SALT	1 TBSP
PEPPER	½ TBSP
BUTTER	2 TBSP
HERBS DE PROVENCE	½ TBSP
THYME	½ TBSP
BLUEBERRY	1 CUP
RASPBERRY	1 CUP
BLACKBERRY	½ CUP
SUGAR	½ CUP

PROCESS

CHICKEN
START WITH THE STEP THAT TAKES THE LONGEST: COOKING YOUR PROTEIN!

Note: Understand that you will get 2 servings per chicken breast; you will slice your chicken breast in half horizontally so there's two equal cuts of chicken.

I. Season with 1 tablespoon of salt, ½ tablespoon of pepper, ½ tablespoon of thyme, and ½ tablespoon of Herbs de Provence.
II. Melt 2 tablespoons of butter and cook each side for 12 minutes while flipping every 3 minutes on medium heat.
III. Once your chicken has finished cooking, set it aside to let it rest for 5 minutes before slicing it to ensure all juices and flavor remain in the chicken.

MIXED BERRY VINAIGRETTE

I. Add ½ cup of blackberries and 1 cup of blueberry and raspberry into a blender along with ½ cup of sugar.
II. Blend for 30 seconds or pulse blend for 5 times.
III. Add 1 teaspoon of balsamic glaze. Continue to blend for another 15 seconds, or 3 pulses, until mixture thickens.
IV. Thinly slice radishes to increase your intake of riboflavin, potassium, and vitamin B-6.

Tip: Chop up some avocados to increase your intake of iron, vitamin D, and zinc. The additional radishes will aid you on your weight loss journey.

VVS | VEGAN, VEGETARIAN, & SALADS

SALADS

APPLE KALE SALAD

SERVING
2 PERSONS

PREP
3 MINUTES

COOK
5 MINUTES

TOTAL
8 MINUTES

FORMULA

INGREDIENTS	AMOUNT
HONEY	2 TBSP
PURPLE ORGANIC KALE	1 BUNCH
APPLE	1
ALMONDS	6
POMEGRANATES	¼ CUP
LEMON	1
WATER	5 CUPS
ICE	2 CUPS

PROCESS

I. Chop 5 leaves of kale.
II. Blanch the kale in 3 cups of hot water for approximately 5 minutes on high heat.
III. Remove the kale and place into a cold ice water bath for 3-5 minutes (two cups of water filled with ice).
IV. Strain excess water from kale.
V. Plate your kale and chop up ¼ of a lemon (extract the seeds), 6 almonds, and ¼ apple for a refreshing garnish.
VI. Add pomegranates for a great source of magnesium, niacin, and energy. Drizzle 2 tbsps of honey.

VVS | VEGAN, VEGETARIAN, & SALADS

SALADS

BLAZIN' BUFFALO SALAD

SERVING
2 PERSONS

PREP
5 MINUTES

COOK
17 MINUTES

TOTAL
22 MINUTES

FORMULA

INGREDIENTS	AMOUNT
CHICKEN BREAST	1
BUFFALO SAUCE	¼ CUP
ROMAINE LETTUCE	1 HEAD
ROMA TOMATOES	2
RED ONION	1
CHEDDAR CHEESE	½ CUP
CUCUMBER	1
CAJUN SEASONING	2 TBSP
GARLIC PEPPER BLEND	2 TBSP
THYME	1 TBSP
RANCH DRY SEASONING	1 TBSP
RANCH	½ CUP
CANOLA OIL	¼ CUP

PROCESS

BLAZIN' SALAD
START WITH THE STEP THAT TAKES THE LONGEST: COOKING YOUR PROTEIN!

I. Butterfly the chicken breast by cutting a horizontal slit along the side into 2 equal portions.

II. Season chicken breasts on each side with 1 tablespoon each of Cajun seasoning and garlic pepper blend, ½ tablespoon of thyme, and 1 tablespoon of ranch dry seasoning powder.

III. Cook the chicken breasts on medium-high heat in a nonstick skillet, or cast iron skillet, for 5 minutes on each side, covered.

IV. Add ¼ cup of oil and continue to cook on medium heat for 2 minutes covered. Flip after the 1 minute mark.

V. Remove from heat. Allow chicken to rest for 5 minutes to ensure that all the juices and flavor remain.

VI. Chop the romaine lettuce, red onion, tomatoes, and cucumbers into a dish. Add cheddar cheese.

VII. Before placing your chicken in your salad, give it a toss in buffalo sauce! Enjoy!

Justin Robinson

VVS | VEGAN, VEGETARIAN, & SALADS

SALADS

QUINOA SALAD BOWL

 **SERVING** 2-4 PERSONS
 **PREP** 8 MINUTES
 COOK 17 MINUTES
 **TOTAL** 25 MINUTES

FORMULA

INGREDIENTS	AMOUNT
QUINOA	½ CUP
BROCCOLI	5 CROWNS
CHICKPEAS	15.5 OZ
RED ONION	1/2
MINCED GARLIC	½ CUP
KALE	5 BRANCHES
RED BELL PEPPER	1
AVOCADO OIL	¾ CUP
RED CABBAGE	1 HEAD
SALT	1 TBSP
CINNAMON	½ TBSP
CAJUN SEASONING	1 TBSP
BUTTER	¼ CUP
WATER	9 CUPS
FETA CHEESE (OPTIONAL)	TO TASTE

PROCESS

CABBAGE/KALE MIXTURE

I. Wash and chop 4 leaves of red cabbage and 5 branches of kale.
II. In a pot, boil kale and cabbage mixture in 4 cups of water for 15 minutes. Drain water.
III. Thinly slice red bell pepper and red onion.
IV. Add ¼ cup of avocado oil into a saucepan. Then, toss in your sliced red onion, red bell pepper, kale, and red cabbage. Finally, add finely chopped broccoli and sauté combination for 7 minutes.
V. Toss in another ¼ cup of avocado oil after 2 minutes.
VI. Optional: Add feta cheese to top off your recipe.

CHICKPEAS

Note: When you pull your chickpeas off, take a bite. They should be slightly firm, but not too mushy.

I. In a pot, bring 3 cups of water to a boil.
II. Strain the canned fluid off your chickpeas and add them to the boiling water.
III. Cook for 5 to 7 minutes, or until you see the outer casing of the chickpeas start to come off.
IV. Strain chickpeas from water.
V. Add ¼ cup of avocado oil, 1 tablespoon of salt, 1 tablespoon of Cajun seasoning and ½ tablespoon of ground cinnamon.
VI. Lightly sauté for 2-3 minutes.

QUINOA

BOIL QUINOA CHICKPEAS AND CABBAGE MIX AT THE SAME TIME.

I. In a pot, bring 2 cups of water to a boil, then, add ½ cup of quinoa.
II. Cook on medium-high heat until all of the water is absorbed.

VVS | VEGAN, VEGETARIAN, & SALADS

SALADS

CHIMICHURRI SALAD

SERVING	PREP	COOK	TOTAL
2 PERSONS	30 MINUTES	10 MINUTES	40 MINUTES

FORMULA

INGREDIENTS	AMOUNT	INGREDIENTS	AMOUNT
STEAK MARINADE		**AVOCADO CREMA**	
FLANK/ SKIRT STEAK	1	AVOCADO	1
LIMES	2	CILANTRO	½ BUNCH
ORANGES	2 - 4	GARLIC	1 CLOVE
ONION	1	LIME JUICE	3 TBSP
CHEF MERITO STEAK AND MEAT SEASONING	2-4 TBSP	SALT	TO TASTE
CILANTRO	1 BUNCH	APPLE CIDER VINEGAR	1 TSP
SALT	1 TBSP	AVOCADO OIL	8 TBSP
PEPPER	1 TBSP		
JALAPEÑOS (OPTIONAL)	1	**SALAD**	
		ARUGULA	1 CUP
		CORN KERNELS	1 CAN
		CHERRY TOMATOES	4
		SPINACH	1 BUNCH
		MEXICAN CHEESE	⅛ CUP
		LIME SALT	1 TSP

VVS | VEGAN, VEGETARIAN, & SALADS

SALADS

CHIMICHURRI SALAD (CONT.)

SERVING
2 PERSONS

PREP
5 MINUTES

COOK
15 MINUTES

TOTAL
20 MINUTES

PROCESS

CHIMICHURRI
ALL OF YOUR FLAVOR WILL COME FROM THE MARINADE'S NATURAL JUICES

I. Wash and dry steak. Lightly season steak with salt and pepper.
II. Generously season with Chef Merito Steak & Meat Seasoning.
III. Combine squeezed lime and orange juices with 1 diced Jalapeño, 1 diced onion and cilantro in a separate bowl.
IV. Bag seasoned meat with citrus mixture. Seal, shake, and store. Marinate for 30 minutes or overnight for best results.
V. Cook each side on high heat for 4 minutes until you see a nice char. It will be a perfect rare inside for your salad.

SALAD

I. Chop fresh cherry tomatoes and combine with arugula, Mexican cheese, and a squeeze of lime.
II. Cook your kernel corn in the same pan the steak was cooked in on high heat for 2 minutes. This ensures the continuous flavor.

AVOCADO CREMA

I. Toss 1 avocado, ½ bunch of cilantro, 1 clove of garlic, 3 tablespoons of lime juice, 1 teaspoon of apple cider vinegar, and 8 tablespoons of avocado oil into a blender.
II. Blend for 1 minute or until desired consistency is achieved.

NOTE: For the final touch, garnish salad with lime salt.

VVS | VEGAN, VEGETARIAN, & SALADS

BRUNCH

CHICKEN AND BEIGNETS

SERVING	PREP	COOK	TOTAL
10 PERSONS	90 MINUTES	20 MINUTES	110 MINUTES

FORMULA

INGREDIENTS	AMOUNT
ACTIVE DRY YEAST	2 ¼ TSP
WARM WATER (110 °F/45 °C)	1 ½ CUPS
WHITE SUGAR	½ CUP
SALT	1 TSP
EGGS	2
EVAPORATED MILK	1 CUP
ALL-PURPOSE FLOUR	7 CUPS
SHORTENING	¼ CUP
VEGETABLE OIL	1 QUART
CONFECTIONERS' SUGAR	¼ CUP
BOURBON WHISKEY	3 SHOTS
APPLE	1
BROWN SUGAR	¼ CUP
SALTED BUTTER	3 TBSP
CINNAMON	1 ½ TBSP
CHICKEN BREASTS	3
GARLIC PEPPER	½ TBSP
CAJUN SEASONING	½ TBSP
RANCH DRY SEASONING MIX	½ TBSP
HONEY	TO TASTE

BOURBON WHISKY SYRUP - HANGOVER PROOF
I. Sauté minced apples in a pan with 3 tablespoons of butter and 1 ½ tablespoons of ground cinnamon.
II. Add 1 handful of brown sugar and 2 shots of Bourbon whisky. Flambe! *Note: Take the 3rd shot!*
III. Reduce to a simmer and let cool for 10 minutes before serving over your chicken and beignets.

PROCESS

BEIGNETS - THE INTRO
I. Add yeast into a large bowl of warm water and mix until water dissolves.
II. Add sugar, salt, eggs and evaporated milk into the bowl. Blend well!
III. Mix in 4 cups of flour and beat until the texture is smooth.
IV. Add the shortening and the remaining 3 cups of flour.
V. Cover tightly and let rise (approximately 45 minutes - 1 hour).

BEIGNETS - THE SEQUEL
SHAKE CONFECTIONERS' SUGAR ON BEIGNETS, AND SERVE WITH YOUR FRIED CHICKEN.
I. Roll out dough 1/8 inch thick (approximately the thickness of 2 quarters stacked). Cut into 2 inch squares.
II. Fry dough squares in canola oil at 356°F.
III. Remove beignets from oil when they begin to puff up and turn golden brown.

CHICKEN
THIS WILL GIVE YOU 8 PORTIONS PER CHICKEN BREAST
I. Cut chicken breast horizontally. Next, cut each section into quarters.
II. Season with garlic pepper, Cajun seasoning, and ranch dry seasoning mix.

Note: Also, use the same seasonings in your flour. Double- Dip if you like it extra crispy!

III. Place chicken breasts in buttermilk and salt mixture. Then, batter in flour and seasoning mixture. Afterwards, fry at 356°F for 8-10 minutes (until golden brown).
IV. Lightly coat fried chicken with a drizzle of honey.
V. Place chicken portions atop beignets and let the good times roll.

BOTOMLEES BRUNCH

BRUNCH
SPICY POTATOES O' BRIEN

SERVING	PREP	COOK	TOTAL
7 PERSONS	10 MINUTES	20 MINUTES	30 MINUTES

FORMULA

INGREDIENTS	AMOUNT
GOLDEN POTATOES	3
YELLOW ONION	½
RED BELL PEPPER	½
SPICY SAUSAGE	1 LINK
GARLIC POWDER	1 TBSP
CAJUN SEASONING	1 TBSP
DRY RANCH SEASONING	1 TBSP
CANOLA OIL	¼ CUP
SALT	TO TASTE
PEPPER	TO TASTE

PROCESS

BRINGING THE HEAT - BRUNCH STYLE

I. Chop three golden potatoes into ½ inch thick portions. Add to a pot.
II. Fill the pot with water until the potatoes are covered.
III. Boil on high heat until water fully evaporates.
IV. Combine your diced onion, diced red bell pepper, and chopped sausage in a skillet. Sauté for 2-3 minutes.
V. Add ¼ cup of oil and potatoes to pepper, onion, and sausage mixture.
VI. Season with garlic powder, Cajun seasoning, and dry ranch seasoning.
VII. Add salt and pepper to your liking.

BRUNCH
CATFISH & GRITS

SERVING
5-6 PERSONS

PREP
5 MINUTES

COOK
15 MINUTES

TOTAL
20 MINUTES

FORMULA

INGREDIENTS	AMOUNT
CATFISH FILETS	6
WATER	3½ CUPS
GRITS	2 CUPS
GOUDA CHEESE	1 BLOCK
HEAVY WHIPPING CREAM	⅔ CUP
CANOLA OIL	¾ GAL
LOUISIANA FISH FRY	3 CUPS
GARLIC POWDER	2 TBSP
ITALIAN CRUSH SEASONING	2 TBSP
CAJUN SEASONING	2 TBSP
BUTTER	2 TBSP
PEPPER	2 TBSP
SALT	2 TBSP

PROCESS

GRITS

I. Boil 3 ½ cups of water. Next, add 2 cups of grits.

Note: Do not add grits until water is at a rolling boil.

II. Stir grits with a whisk to prevent clumps.

III. Once water is absorbed, reduce heat to a low setting, and continuously whisk when removing the pot from the eye (5 seconds on... 10 seconds off) until grits thicken.

IV. Add ⅓ cup of heavy whipping cream while repeating the stirring cycle from Step 3.

V. Add an additional ⅓ cup of heavy whipping cream once previous whipping cream has been stirred in.

VI. Add 2 tablespoons of each of the following: butter, salt, and pepper.

VII. Next, add one cup of shredded Gouda cheese. Mix thoroughly. Allow grits to rest.

CATFISH

I. Season catfish with garlic powder, Italian crush seasoning, and Cajun seasoning.

II. Batter in Louisiana Fish Fry mix.

III. Fry at 340°F for 8-10 minutes until golden brown.

Justin Robinson

BOTOMLEES BRUNCH

EGGS 5 WAYS

BACON EGG & CHEESE SANDWICH

SERVING
2 PERSONS

PREP
2 MINUTES

COOK
5 MINUTES

TOTAL
7 MINUTES

FORMULA

INGREDIENTS	AMOUNT
EGGS	3
MILK	SPLASH
BACON	2 STRIPS
CHEDDAR	¼ CUP
BUTTER	1 ½ TBSP
ENGLISH MUFFINS	2
SALT	TO TASTE
PEPPER	TO TASTE

PROCESS

EGG-CEPTIONAL

I. Coat the English muffins with butter.
II. Toast muffins in the oven on broil face up until desired crust is achieved (30 seconds-1 minute).
III. Remove English muffins. Cut 2 bacon strips in half, and place them in the oven on broil until desired crisp is achieved (approximately 3-4 minutes).
IV. Crack 3 eggs in a bowl and add a splash of milk. Whisk!
V. Cook in a non-stick skillet on medium heat.
VI. The trick is to place the skillet on the eye for 30 seconds then 10 seconds off. Fold egg in mixture repeatedly using a folding spatula until desired texture is achieved.
VII. Toss in 1 tablespoon of butter and ¼ cup of cheddar cheese and fold into eggs.
VIII. Build your English muffin masterpiece!

Note

THIS IS A QUICK AND EASY TIME SAVER TO ALLOW YOU TO START YOUR DAY THE RIGHT WAY! WHETHER IT'S PREPPING FOR THE WEEK OR FOR BRUNCH.

Justin Robinson

BOTOMLEES BRUNCH

EGGS 5 WAYS

PERFECTLY SCRAMBLED

SERVING — 4 PERSONS
PREP — 1 MINUTE
COOK — 2 MINUTES
TOTAL — 3 MINUTES

FORMULA

INGREDIENTS	AMOUNT
EGGS	5
MILK	SPLASH
CAJUN SEASONING	1 TBSP
PEPPER	½ TBSP
BUTTER	1 TBSP
CHIVES	1 BUNCH

PROCESS

EGG-ECUTE

I. Crack 5 eggs in a bowl and add a splash of milk.
II. Wrist work! (Whisk)
III. Cook in a non-stick skillet on medium heat.
IV. The trick is place the skillet on the eye for 30 seconds, then 10 seconds off, while using a folding spatula to fold in the egg mixture repeatedly.
V. Season with pepper and Cajun seasoning, and add 1 tablespoon of butter.
VI. Garnish your Perfectly Scrambled Eggs with chives!

BOTOMLEES BRUNCH

EGGS 5 WAYS

SUNNY SIDE UP ON AVOCADO TOAST

SERVING
2 PERSONS

PREP
3 MINUTES

COOK
7 MINUTES

TOTAL
10 MINUTES

FORMULA

INGREDIENTS	AMOUNT
EGGS	2
AVOCADO	1
CIABATTA BREAD	2 HALVES
PEPPER	¼ CUP
SALT	TO TASTE
RED PEPPER FLAKES	TO TASTE
BUTTER	2 TBSP
WATER	⅔ CUP

PROCESS

2 EGGS ARE BETTER THAN 1!

I. Coat your ciabatta bread with butter.
II. Lightly toast the bread in a nonstick skillet, face down, until desired buttery crust is achieved. Set your ciabatta toast aside.
III. Slice an avocado in half and extract seed; make thin slits in avocado. Spoon and lay each half accordingly per slice of bread.
IV. Spray cooking oil onto a nonstick skillet. Then add 2 tablespoons of butter on medium heat.
V. Crack 2 eggs into a skillet once butter melts.
VI. Be sure to crack eggs close to the pan; this way the yolk doesn't break form.
- Cook for 1 minute uncovered.
- Add ⅓ cup of water gently around the eggs. Cover for 30 seconds.
- Uncover and cook for another minute.
- Add ⅓ cup of water, cover, and cook for 30 seconds.
- Remove covering and cook for 1 minute.

Note: This is how you cook the perfect sunny side up and ensure that the egg white is fully cooked.

VII. Lay sunny side up egg on the avocado toast. Crack salt, pepper, and red pepper flakes for taste!

Justin Robinson

BOTOMLEES BRUNCH

EGGS 5 WAYS

TRUFFLE HOT SAUCE POACHED EGGS BENEDICT

SERVING
2 PERSONS

PREP
1 MINUTE

COOK
4 MINUTES

TOTAL
5 MINUTES

FORMULA

INGREDIENTS	AMOUNT
EGGS	2
HAM	2 SLICES
BACON	2 STRIPS
ENGLISH MUFFIN	1
TRUFFLE HOT SAUCE	TO TASTE
BUTTER	1 TBSP
SALT	TO TASTE
PEPPER	TO TASTE
WATER	3 CUPS

PROCESS

EGG-TREME HEAT - MUFFIN

I. Halve the English muffin. Coat the inside halves with butter.

II. Toast muffins in the oven on broil face up until desired crust is achieved (30-60 seconds).

III. Remove the English muffins. Cut 2 bacon strips in half. Broil the bacon strips and a thick slice of ham in the oven until desired crust is achieved (3-4 minutes).

EGGS

I. In a pot, boil 3 cups of water.

II. Create a vortex in the boiling water by whisking counter-clock wise around the pot.

III. Gently crack and lay 2 eggs dead center of the water vortex and watch them swirl around.

Note: The yolk will begin to cook, and after 45-60 seconds, the perfect poached egg will be formed.

IV. Carefully spoon off excess egg white and pull cooked yolk from the boiling pot. Lay onto your English muffin.

V. Crack with salt and pepper to taste. Drizzle desired sauce whether its hollandaise or, in this case, a black truffle infused hot sauce.

Note: COOKING YOUR BREAD AND BACON IN THE OVEN IS A QUICK AND EASY TIME SAVER TO ALLOW YOU TO START ON YOUR EGGS!

BOTOMLEES BRUNCH

EGGS 5 WAYS

MEAT LOVERS CRUSTLESS QUICHE

SERVING
8 PERSONS

PREP
10 MINUTES

COOK
50 MINUTES

TOTAL
60 MINUTES

FORMULA

INGREDIENTS	AMOUNT
EGGS	8
MILK	¼ cup
BACON	2 STRIPS
HAM	2 SLICES
CHEDDAR CHEESE	¼ CUP
GROUND ITALIAN SAUSAGE	¼ LB
GREEN ONION	TO TASTE
SPINACH	½ CUP
RED ONIONS	½
RED BELL PEPPER	1
CAJUN SEASONING	1 TBSP
SALT	1 TBSP
PEPPER	1 TBSP
CAYENNE PEPPER	¼ TBSP
PARSLEY	1 TBSP

PROCESS

EGG-CELLENT QUICHE

I. Crack 8 eggs and whisk in a bowl.
II. Combine 1 tablespoon of Cajun Seasoning, 1 tablespoon of salt, 1 tablespoon of pepper, ¼ tablespoon of Cayenne pepper and 1 tablespoon of parsley into the bowl of eggs.
III. Add ½ minced red onion, ½ cup of freshly chopped spinach, and 1 diced red bell pepper into the mixture.
IV. Cook ¼ lb ground Italian sausage in a nonstick skillet until it browns (approximately 8 to 10 minutes). Break down the clusters of meat in the pan and add them into the mixture.
V. Pour the mixture into a baking bowl along with ¼ cup of cheddar cheese.
VI. Dice 2 slices of ham and 2 strips of bacon. Brown each in a non stick skillet over medium-high heat.
VII. Coat the baking pan with nonstick spray. Transfer contents from the bowl into a 3 quart baking pan. Top the diced ham and bacon over the quiche.
VIII. Bake in the oven at 385°F for 40-45 minutes.

BOTOMLEES BRUNCH

SOUTHERN

OSPITALITY

SOUTHERN HOSPITALITY

MAC ATTACK

SERVING	PREP	COOK	TOTAL
6 PERSONS	1 MINUTE	20 MINUTES	21 MINUTES

FORMULA

INGREDIENTS	AMOUNT
ELBOW NOODLES	½ LB
HEAVY WHIPPING CREAM	½ CUP
CHEDDAR JACK CHEESE	¼ CUP
GOUDA CHEESE	¼ CUP
CHEDDAR CHEESE	¼ CUP
BACON BITS	TO TASTE
PARSLEY	TO TASTE
SALT	1 TBSP
PEPPER	1 TBSP
GARLIC POWDER	1 TBSP
CAJUN SEASONING	1 TBSP

PROCESS

I. Bring 4 cups of water to a rolling boil in a pot. Pour in ½ pound of elbow noodles and boil for 5-10 minutes.

II. Pour ½ cup of heavy whipping cream into a seperate sauce pot on medium-high heat. Allow to simmer.

III. Caution: The cream may boil out of the pot so keep a close eye on it.

IV. Season the cream with salt, pepper, garlic powder, and Cajun seasoning-- 1 tablespoon of each. Add in ¼ cup of cheddar cheese and whisk until fully combined. Don't be afraid to taste test in order to ensure the flavor of the base is to your liking.

V. Combine sauce and noodles, and mix the combination thoroughly. Then add ¼ cup of shredded gouda cheese and mix.

VI. Cover the top of your Mac Attack with cheddar jack cheese and cheddar cheese.

VII. Lastly, place under broil until a crisp cheese crust is achieved (1-3 min.)

SOUTHERN HOSPITALITY

GUMBO

SERVING
15+ PERSONS

PREP
20 MINUTES

COOK
60 MINUTES

TOTAL
80 MINUTES

FORMULA

INGREDIENTS	AMOUNT
CELERY STICKS	3
YELLOW ONION	1
GREEN BELL PEPPER	1
FLOUR	½ CUP
CHICKEN BOUILLON CUBE	1
CHICKEN STOCK	4 QT
PARSLEY	1 BUNCH
GUMBO FILE POWDER	1 TBSP
CHOPPED TOMATOES	1 CAN
BUTTER	½ CUP
BAY LEAVES	2
CHICKEN THIGHS	8
SPICY SAUSAGE	1 LB
CAJUN SEASONING	2 TBSP
OIL	¼ CUP
GARLIC POWDER	2 TBSP
SALT	4 TBSP
PEPPER	2 TBSP

PROCESS

COOKING OFF PROTEINS – SEASON/SLICE/SAUTÉ

I. Season chicken thighs with the same seasoning as Step 1 of the fried chicken recipe on page (41).

II. In a non-stick skillet, cook each side for 8-10 minutes in ¼ cup of canola oil, then finish the chicken off in the oven at 400°F for 10 minutes.

III. Afterwards, remove the chicken from the oven and let it sit for 7 minutes. Chop the meat off the bone. Set chopped chicken aside to cool off.

IV. The chicken will not be fully cooked through, but don't worry you still have an hour in the gumbo broth. This will prevent your chicken from drying out.

V. Cook the sliced sausage in the same pan your chicken was in for 4 minutes on high heat; then, set meat aside along with chicken.

VI. DO NOT DRAIN YOUR GREASE IT WILL BE USED TO ASSIST YOU WHEN MAKING YOUR ROUX.

VII. In a large pot, combine ½ cup of butter, oil from the previous chicken and sausage, and ½ cup flour. Cook over medium heat while frequently stirring with a whisk to make a dark brown roux. You have to continue to stir every 30-60 seconds to prevent the roux from burning (takes approx 12-15 mins).

VIII. Once you achieve your perfect roux, toss in the celery, bell pepper, onion, Cajun seasoning, salt, and pepper. Cook for 8 to 10 minutes. Then, add in your can of chopped tomatoes, sliced Andouille sausage and chicken. Cook for an additional 5 minutes. Stir occasionally.

IX. Toss in 2 bay leaves, 2 tablespoons of Cajun seasoning, 1 tablespoon of gumbo file, 2 tablespoons of garlic powder, and 4 quarts of chicken stock. Bring to a boil and reduce the heat to a simmer for 50 minutes. Stir. taste... and season more to your liking if need be.

X. Use a 2:1 ratio (2 cups of water per 1 cup of rice). Boil rice over medium-high heat. Stir occasionally every 5 to 6 minutes.

XI. Season rice with 4 tablespoons of salt and 2 tablespoons of pepper. Once water is fully absorbed, toss in 1 tablespoon of butter and stir!

Justin Robinson

SOUTHERN HOSPITALITY

GLORIA GREENS

SERVING
5-6 PERSONS

PREP
10 MINUTES

COOK
40 MINUTES

TOTAL
50 MINUTES

FORMULA

INGREDIENTS	AMOUNT
COLLARD GREENS	2 BUNCHES
ONION	1
TURKEY NECK	1
CHICKEN BOUILLON CUBE	1
CHICKEN STOCK	4 CUPS
OIL	¼ CUP
SALT	1 TBSP
PEPPER	2 TBSP

PROCESS

"YOU GOTTA WASH EACH OF THEM LEAVES OFF TO GET ALL THE JUNK OFF." - GRANDMA
SO WE'RE GONNA DO EXACTLY WHAT MY GRANDMA SAID!

I. Wash your leaves and peel them off the stem.
II. Roll them into a big cigar-like shape.
III. Chop the greens in ½ inch segments.
IV. In a large pot, sauté your diced onion and turkey neck with ¼ cup of oil for 3-5 minutes on medium heat..
V. Season with 1 tablespoon of salt and 2 tablespoons of pepper.
VI. Add your chopped greens, diced onions, and turkey neck into a pot.
VII. Pour in 4 cups of chicken stock and toss in your bouillon cube. Stir, and cover
VIII. Cook for 40 minutes until the greens are tender. Season to taste!

HOME MADE
SIGNATURE
RECIPE
Grandma Gloria

SOUTHERN HOSPITALITY

APPLE POT PIE

SERVING
2 PERSONS

PREP
5 MINUTES

COOK
35 MINUTES

TOTAL
40 MINUTES

FORMULA

INGREDIENTS	AMOUNT
FUJI APPLE	1
BUTTER	4 TBSP
OIL	¼ CUP
CARAMEL	2½ TBSP
BROWN SUGAR	⅔ CUP
VANILLA EXTRACT	4 TBSP
GROUND CINNAMON	6 TBSP
APPLE PIE SEASONING	3 TBSP
PIE CRUST	1

PROCESS

SWEET AS PIE

I. Chop 1 Fuji apple into chunks.
II. Add the apple chunks and 2 cups of water into a saucepan. Cook until water evaporates.
III. Add ¼ cup of oil with 4 tablespoons of butter after the water has evaporated from the saucepan.
IV. Sauté for 3-4 minutes.
V. Add ⅔ cups of brown sugar, 4 tablespoons of vanilla extract, 6 tablespoons of ground cinnamon, and 3 tablespoons of apple pie seasoning to the apples. Continue to sauté for an additional 2-3 minutes.
VI. Add in a 5-second squeeze of caramel.
VII. Continue to work the ingredients into the apples.
VIII. Place your apple mixture to the side. Let them cool for 2-3 minutes.
IX. Stuff the pie crust into a soufflé bowl.
X. Pour apple pie mixture into the crust and fold pastry dough over itself to create your apple pot pie.
XI. Place in the oven at 425°F for 15-20 minutes.
XII. Garnish with apple cinnamon.

SOUTHERN HOSPITALITY

JALAPENO CAST IRON CORNBREAD

SERVING
10-12 PERSONS

PREP
5 MINUTES

COOK
40 MINUTES

TOTAL
45 MINUTES

FORMULA

INGREDIENTS	AMOUNT
JALAPENOS	1
FLOUR	2 CUPS
CORNMEAL	1 CUP
CREAM OF CORN	¼ CUP
SUGAR	1 ½ CUP
BAKING POWDER	1 ¼ TBSP
MELTED BUTTER	½ CUP
SALT	PINCH
CUP OF CANOLA OIL	½ CUP
CUP MILK	1 ¼ CUP
BACON GREASE	3 TBSP
EGGS	3

PROCESS

CORNBREAD REIMAGINED

I. Grease cast iron skillet with bacon grease.
II. Add 1 fresh chopped jalapeno, ¼ cup of cream of corn, 2 cups of flour, 1 cup of cornmeal, 1 ½ cups of sugar, 1 ¼ tablespoons of baking powder, a pinch of salt, ½ cup of melted butter, ½ cup of canola oil, 1 ¼ cups of milk, 3 eggs, and a drizzle of honey to a bowl. Whisk!
III. Pour the contents into a cast iron skillet.
IV. Bake at 325°F for 40 minutes.

Justin Robinson

SOUTHERN HOSPITALITY

TRAEGER SMOKED CHICKEN

SERVING	PREP	COOK	TOTAL
10-12 PERSONS	10 MINUTES	80 MINUTES	90 MINUTES

FORMULA

INGREDIENTS	AMOUNT
HONEY	TO TASTE
CHICKEN LEGS, THIGHS, WINGS	5 LBS
GARLIC PEPPER	1 ½ TBSP
CAJUN SEASONING	1 ½ TBSP
RANCH DRY SEASONING MIX	1 ½ TBSP
SALT	PINCH
PEPPER	PINCH
TRAEGER CHICKEN RUB	½ TBSP

PROCESS

I. Preheat Traeger Grill to 310°F.
II. Season chicken with 1 ½ tablespoon of garlic pepper, 1 ½ tablespoon of Cajun seasoning, 1 ½ tablespoon of ranch dry seasoning mix, 1 pinch of salt, 1 pinch of pepper, and ½ tablespoon of Trager chicken rub.
III. Place chicken on grill for 1 hour at 310°F.
IV. Turn grill up to 420°F and cook for an additional 20 minutes.

Note: You may use your oven as an alternative, however, to savor the flavor you gotta' use a Traeger! For this reason, I highly recommend you join #TraegerNation!

BREAKI

BREAK BREAD

CINNAMON ROLLS

SERVING — 8-12 PERSONS
PREP — 100 MINUTES
COOK — 20 MINUTES
TOTAL — 120 MINUTES

FORMULA

INGREDIENTS	AMOUNT
UNSALTED BUTTER	½ CUP
MILK	4 TBSP
YEAST	1 TBSP
POWDERED SUGAR	1 CUP
BROWN SUGAR	1 ¼ CUPS
SUGAR	2 TBSP
FLOUR	3 CUPS
EGGS	2
SALT	1 PINCH
GROUND CINNAMON	7-8 TBSP
BROWN SUGAR	¾ CUPS
VANILLA EXTRACT	1 TBSP
SALTED BUTTER	2 TBSP

FILLING - THE SUGAR RUSH YOU NEED!

I. Melt ¼ cup of unsalted butter, ¾ cup of brown sugar, and 4 tablespoons of ground cinnamon.

ICING - TIME FOR THE DRIP

I. Combine 1 cup of powdered sugar, 2 tablespoons of butter, 1 tablespoon of vanilla extract, and 2 tablespoons of milk in a bowl. Mix to form the perfect glaze for your cinnamon rolls!

PROCESS

DOUGH - ROLLING IN THE DOUGH

I. Mix 2 tablespoons of milk, 2 eggs, ¼ cup of melted butter, 2 tablespoons of sugar, a pinch of salt, and 1 tablespoon of yeast in a large bowl for 5 minutes or until mixture begins to foam.

II. This is a marathon, not a sprint. For your mixer, start with a low setting and work your way up to a high setting. Incrementally, add 3 cups of flour to the mixture.

III. Increase mixing speed until the dough texture is soft, but not too sticky to handle.

IV. Knead dough on a floured surface and form into a ball.

V. Transfer dough into a separate and lightly greased mixing bowl.

VI. Cover, and let rise for 1 hour.

Note: Be sure to place in a warm area. This will allow the dough to double in size.

THE ROLLOUT - JACKPOT

I. Roll out dough until it's ¼ inch thick.

II. Cut dough into a rectangle.

III. Rub melted butter over dough.

IV. Rub brown sugar on top of dough with fingers.

V. Roll your dough in a pinwheel motion.

VI. Once dough is rolled, cut cinnamon roll portions to your liking.

VII. Line up cinnamon rolls in a baking dish, and let rise for 30 minutes.

VIII. Bake at 350°F for 17-21 minutes.

SLIDERS/BURGERS

THE GOOD BURGER

SERVING
2 PERSONS

PREP
5 MINUTES

COOK
16 MINUTES

TOTAL
21 MINUTES

FORMULA

INGREDIENTS	AMOUNT
CHEDDAR CHEESE	4 SLICES
BRIOCHE BUNS	2
LETTUCE	4 LEAVES
BACON	8 SLICES
TOMATO	½
ONION	1
GROUND BEEF	1 LB
BLACK PEPPER	1 TBSP
ONION POWDER	1 TBSP
KINDERS SEASONING	1 TBSP
GARLIC PEPPER	1 TBSP
HERBS DE PROVENCE	1 TBSP
RANCH DRY SEASONING	1 TBSP
DALE'S MARINADE	2 TBSP
EGGS	1
ITALIAN BREAD CRUMBS	4 TBSP

PROCESS

WELCOME TO THE GOOD BURGER

I. Combine 1 pound of ground beef with 1 tablespoon of each of the following: black pepper, onion powder, Kinder's Buttery Steak House seasoning, garlic pepper, Herbs de Provence, and ranch dry seasoning. Then add 2 tablespoons of Dale's Marinade, 4 tablespoons of Italian bread crumbs, and 1 egg.

II. No fancy trick here; use hands to form 2 half pound patties!

III. If you're not sure what a half pound looks like, just spread meat on a flat surface and divide into 2 portions.

IV. Cook each side of the burgers on high heat for 5 minutes in a cast iron skillet.

V. Finish off burgers in the oven at 375°F for an additional 6 minutes.

VI. Set aside burgers and allow them to rest in order to lock in all juices.

TRAEGER COOK

I. Cook in Traeger at 375°F for 15 minutes.

II. Dress burger with toppings of your choice, and serve with an ice cold beer!

BREAKING BREAD

SLIDERS/BURGERS

PRIME TIME

SERVING
1-2 PERSONS

PREP
3 MINUTES

COOK
22 MINUTES

TOTAL
25 MINUTES

FORMULA

INGREDIENTS	AMOUNT
SHAVED PRIME RIB	1 RIBEYE
PROVOLONE CHEESE	3 SLICES
LONG PICKLES	3
ARUGULA	1 TBSP
MULTIGRAIN BAGUETTE	1
YELLOW ONIONS	½
MUSHROOMS	¼ CUP
DALE'S MARINADE	1 TBSP
BUTTER	5 TBSP
FLOUR	2 TBSP
GARLIC	1 TBSP
ITALIAN SEASONING	3 TBSP
RANCH DRY SEASONING	1 TBSP
BLACK PEPPER	1 TBSP
SALT	1 TBSP

PROCESS

STEAK- RIBEYE IS OUR CHOICE OF CUT.
I. Season ribeye with 1 tablespoon of the following: garlic, ranch dry seasoning, black pepper, salt, and crushed Italian seasoning. Season steak inside the cast iron skillet to transfer the flavor to the Au jus.
II. Place the steak in the oven at 375°F for 6 minutes. Flip ribeye at 3 minutes.
III. Remove steak and allow it to rest.

TAKE IT TO THE TRAEGER
I. Set it and forget it at 375°F for 6 minutes. Toast baguette at 425 °F until desired crust is achieved

AU JUS- DOUBLE-DIPPING WITH ELEGANCE.
I. Combine 3 tablespoons of butter, 2 tablespoons of all-purpose flour, 1 tablespoon of Dale's Marinade and ¼ cup of red wine into the same cast iron skillet that the ribeye was in.
II. Reduce on medium-heat for 5 minutes.
III. Remove Au Jus mixture from skillet. For the toppings, sauté ½ sliced onion and ¼ cup of mushrooms on high heat until caramelized (Approximately 3-5 minutes).

BAGUETTE- THE ASSEMBLY
I. Paint the inside halves of the baguettes with 2 tablespoons of butter and Italian seasoning mixture.
II. Broil until desired crust is achieved.
III. Remove baguettes and add provolone cheese, onions, and mushrooms. Place baguette back under a broil to melt and create the base for your prime rib sandwich.
IV. Thinly shave ribeye with a sharp knife. Stack shavings on base. Garnish with arugula and pickles.

BREAKING BREAD

SLIDERS/BURGERS

SALMON BURGER

SERVING	**PREP**	**COOK**	**TOTAL**
4-8 PERSONS	10 MINUTES	11 MINUTES	21 MINUTES

FORMULA

INGREDIENTS	AMOUNT
SALMON FILETS	2
CILANTRO	1/4 CUP
ARUGULA	1 CUP
TOMATO	1
RED ONION	½
RED BELL PEPPER	½
LIME	½
BRIOCHE BUN	4 - 8
HONEY	2 TBSP
BUTTER	¼ CUP
CAJUN SEASONING	2 TBSP
RED PEPPER FLAKES	½ TBSP
ITALIAN CRUSHED SEASONING	2 TBSP
ORANGE PEEL	1 TBSP
GROUND CINNAMON	½ TBSP
GROUND GINGER	1 TBSP

PROCESS

SALMON BURGERS

I. Chop ½ red bell pepper, ½ red onion, a handful of cilantro, and 2 salmon filets.
II. Combine chopped ingredients into a blender with half a squeeze of lime.
III. Pulse until mixture imitates ground meat to form patties.
IV. Cook for 3 minutes on each side.
V. Finish off in the oven at 375°F for 5 minutes.

HONEY BUTTER

I. Combine ½ tablespoon of ground cinnamon, 2 tablespoons of honey, and a ¼ cup of butter at room temperature.

BRIOCHE BUN- THE ASSEMBLY

I. Paint honey butter on the inside of the bun, and lightly toast bread in a cast iron skillet on medium-high heat (3-5 minutes).
II. Piece together salmon, tomato, arugula, and more honey butter if you love it as much as I do.

SLIDERS/BURGERS

BLACK BEAN BURGER

SERVING
4-8 PERSONS

PREP
10 MINUTES

COOK
42 MINUTES

TOTAL
52 MINUTES

FORMULA

INGREDIENTS	AMOUNT
BLACK BEANS (15.5 OZ EACH)	4
BRIOCHE BUN	4-8
CILANTRO	1 BUNCH
RED BELL PEPPER	1
CORN	8 OZ
AVOCADO	½
GARLIC	1 TBSP
ONION	½
DALE'S MARINADE	3 TBSP
PAPRIKA	1 TBSP
SMOKED GOUDA CHEESE	¼ CUP
PROVOLONE CHEESE	4 SLICES
EGGS	2
APPLE CIDER VINEGAR	½ CUP
CAJUN SEASONING	1 TBSP

PROCESS

BEGIN WITH THE BEANS!

I. Drain bean juice from the can, and place beans on a cooking sheet. Broil for 20 minutes. The goal is to dehydrate the beans.

II. Chop ½ onion, 1 red bell pepper, and 1 bunch of cilantro.

III. Combine the chopped onion, bell pepper, and cilantro with roasted black beans, 2 eggs, 3 tablespoons of Dale's Marinade, and 1 tablespoon of each of the following: salt, pepper, garlic powder, paprika and Cajun seasoning, in a blender and pulse until fully combined.

IV. Form patties with the Step 3 mixture and cook on med-high heat with ¼ cup of canola oil for 10-12 mins.

V. Finish off in the oven at 375 °F for 5 minutes.

ASSEMBLE- GO BIG OR GO HOME!

I. Lightly coat the inside of the bun with butter and toast in a skillet for 3-5 minutes.

II. Assemble your black bean burger (In this case, a double-decker).

III. For topping assembly, slice half an avocado, and to pickle your red onions, soak them in ½ cup of apple cider vinegar for 30-60 minutes.

Note: You can adjust the acidity by adding ½ tablespoon of salt and 1 tablespoon of sugar.

SLIDERS/BURGERS

BUFFALO CHICKEN SLIDERS

SERVING — 4-8 PERSONS
PREP — 20 MINUTES
COOK — 40 MINUTES
TOTAL — 60 MINUTES

FORMULA

INGREDIENTS	AMOUNT
BRIOCHE BUNS	4-8
CHICKEN THIGHS	2
PEPPER JACK CHEESE	¼ LB
PICKLE	TO TASTE
YELLOW ONION	½
GARLIC PEPPER	2 TBSP
CAJUN SEASONING	2 TBSP
RANCH DRY SEASONING	2 TBSP
BUFFALO SAUCE (HOT SAUCE & BUTTER)	2 CUPS
CAULIFLOWER (SUBSTITUTE)	1

- 1 CHICKEN THIGH = 3 SLIDERS
- 1 CAULIFLOWER HEAD = 8 SLIDERS

PROCESS

BANGIN' BUFFALO

I. Season chicken thighs with garlic pepper, Cajun seasoning, and ranch dry seasoning mix.
II. Note: For a vegan alternative, use cauliflower in the following recipe.
III. Place in a baking dish and cover with aluminum foil.
IV. Cook at 425 °F for 35-40 minutes.
V. Remove chicken thighs, and set them aside for 10 minutes.
VI. Chop the meat off the bone and portion into slider sizes.
VII. Create the sauce (1 cup of hot sauce, 1 cup of softened butter, and 1 teaspoon of Dale's Marinade). Apply to meat.
VIII. In a skillet, sauté half an onion with a drizzle of oil for 3-5 minutes until caramelized.
IX. Remove onions and toast buns in the same skillet immediately afterward until desired crust is achieved.
X. Assemble sliders with buffalo chicken, pepper jack cheese, caramelized onions, and a pickle slice.

Justin Robinson

NEST

JAMBALAYA

CHICKEN

MEAT LOVERS

FLATBREADS

MARGHERITA

SERVING
1-3 PERSONS

PREP
15 MINUTES

COOK
75 MINUTES

TOTAL
90 MINUTES

FORMULA

INGREDIENTS	AMOUNT
WARM WATER	⅓ CUP
SALT	PINCH
OIL	1 TSP
DRY YEAST	1 TSP
SUGAR	PINCH
ALL PURPOSE FLOUR	¾ CUP
TOMATOES	TO TASTE
BASIL	TO TASTE
MOZZARELLA CHUNKS	TO TASTE
MARINARA SAUCE	TO TASTE
BALSAMIC DRIZZLE	TO TASTE

PROCESS

I. Thoroughly combine the following dough ingredients: 1/3 cup of warm water, pinch of salt, 1 teaspoon of oil, 1 teaspoon of dry yeast, pinch of sugar, and 3/4 cup of all-purpose flour.

II. Let dough rise for an hour.

III. Roll out the dough into desired flatbread shape and base the dough with butter and Italian crushed seasoning.

IV. Layer with marinara.

V. Slice tomatoes, chop mozzarella chunks, and design the pizza to your liking.

VI. Cook in the oven or Traeger at 450°F for 10-15 minutes.

VII. Slice fresh basil leaves and garnish pizza. Afterwards, drizzle pizza with balsamic glaze.

BREAKING BREAD

FLATBREADS
MEATLOVERS

SERVING
1-3 PERSONS

PREP
15 MINUTES

COOK
75 MINUTES

TOTAL
90 MINUTES

FORMULA

INGREDIENTS	AMOUNT
WARM WATER	⅓ CUP
SALT	PINCH
OIL	1 TSP
DRY YEAST	1 TSP
SUGAR	PINCH
ALL PURPOSE FLOUR	¾ CUP
ITALIAN SAUSAGE	TO TASTE
BACON	TO TASTE
PEPPERONI	TO TASTE
HAM	TO TASTE
MARINARA SAUCE	TO TASTE
MOZZARELLA CHEESE	TO TASTE

PROCESS

I. Thoroughly combine the following dough ingredients: 1/3 cup of warm water, pinch of salt, 1 teaspoon of oil, 1 teaspoon of dry yeast, pinch of sugar, and 3/4 cup of all-purpose flour.

II. Let dough rise for an hour. While dough is rising, start cooking your meat.

III. Thinly chop 2 slices of bacon, 2 slices of thick cut ham, and ⅓ pound of Italian sausage. Cook until meat browns.

IV. Roll out the dough into desired flatbread shape and base the dough with butter and italian crushed seasoning.

V. Layer with marinara and mozzarella cheese.

VI. Design pizza to your liking.

VII. Cook in the oven or Traeger at 450°F for 10-15 minutes.

BREAKING BREAD

FLATBREADS
HAWAIIAN

SERVING	**PREP**	**COOK**	**TOTAL**
1-3 PERSONS	15 MINUTES	75 MINUTES	90 MINUTES

FORMULA

INGREDIENTS	AMOUNT
WARM WATER	⅓ CUP
SALT	PINCH
OIL	1 TSP
DRY YEAST	1 TSP
SUGAR	PINCH
ALL PURPOSE FLOUR	¾ CUP
PINEAPPLE	TO TASTE
HAM	TO TASTE
SPINACH	TO TASTE
BBQ DRIZZLE	TO TASTE
MARINARA SAUCE	TO TASTE
MOZZARELLA CHEESE	TO TASTE

PROCESS

I. Thoroughly combine the following dough ingredients: 1/3 cup of warm water, pinch of salt, 1 teaspoon of oil, 1 teaspoon of dry yeast, pinch of sugar, and 3/4 cup of all-purpose flour.

II. Let dough rise for an hour.

III. Roll out the dough into desired flatbread shape and base the dough with butter and Italian crushed seasoning.

IV. Layer with marinara and mozzarella cheese.

V. Design pizza to your liking with sliced ham, pineapple, and spinach leaves.

VI. Cook in the oven or Traeger at 450°F for 10-15 minutes.

VII. Drizzle with BBQ sauce.

FLATBREADS
BUFFALO CHICKEN

SERVING	PREP	COOK	TOTAL
1-3 PERSONS	15 MINUTES	75 MINUTES	90 MINUTES

FORMULA

INGREDIENTS	AMOUNT
WARM WATER	⅓ CUP
SALT	½ TBSP
OLIVE OIL	¼ CUP
DRY YEAST	1 TSP
SUGAR	PINCH
ALL PURPOSE FLOUR	¾ CUP
CHICKEN BREAST	½
JALAPENO	TO TASTE
BUFFALO SAUCE	TO TASTE
RED ONION	⅓
MARINARA SAUCE	TO TASTE
MOZZARELLA CHEESE	TO TASTE
KICK'N CHICKEN	½ TBSP
PEPPER	1 TBSP
GARLIC POWDER	1 TBSP
DALE'S MARINADE	1 TSP
BUTTER	1 CUP

PROCESS

I. Thoroughly combine the following dough ingredients: 1/3 cup of warm water, pinch of salt, 1 teaspoon of oil, 1 teaspoon of dry yeast, pinch of sugar, and 3/4 cup of all-purpose flour.

II. Let dough rise for an hour. Cook toppings in the meantime.

III. Season chopped chicken breast with 1 tablespoon of pepper, and garlic powder and ½ tablespoon of salt and Kick'n Chicken.

IV. Add ¼ cup of olive oil in a skillet and saute the chopped chicken and sliced red onion for 6-8 minutes.

V. The chicken will finish cooking as a topping in the oven/Traeger.

VI. Roll out the dough into desired flatbread shape and base the dough with butter and Italian crushed seasoning.

VII. Layer with marinara and mozzarella cheese.

VIII. Design pizza to your liking, along with minced jalapeno pepper.

IX. Cook in the oven or Traeger at 450°F for 10-15 minutes.

X. Drizzle with buffalo sauce-- 1 cup of hot sauce, 1 cup of softened butter, and 1 teaspoon of Dale's Marinade.

FLATBREADS
SOUTHWEST PIZZA

SERVING — 1-3 PERSONS
PREP — 15 MINUTES
COOK — 75 MINUTES
TOTAL — 90 MINUTES

FORMULA

INGREDIENTS	AMOUNT
WATER	⅓ CUP
SALT	PINCH
OIL	1 TSP
DRY YEAST	1 TSP
SUGAR	PINCH
ALL PURPOSE FLOUR	¾ CUP
RED ONIONS	TO TASTE
ORANGE BELL PEPPER	TO TASTE
FLANK STEAK	¼ LB
MONTEREY JACK	TO TASTE
RED BELL PEPPER	1
AVOCADO	½
CILANTRO	BUNCH
GARLIC	1 CLOVE
LIME JUICE	3 TBSP
APPLE CIDER VINEGAR	1 TBSP
AVOCADO OIL	TO TASTE
MARINARA SAUCE	TO TASTE
MOZZARELLA CHEESE	TO TASTE
CHEF MERITOS SEASONING	2 TBSP
PEPPER	1 TSP

PROCESS

I. Thoroughly combine the following dough ingredients: 1/3 cup of warm water, pinch of salt, 1 teaspoon of oil, 1 teaspoon of dry yeast, pinch of sugar, and 3/4 cup of all-purpose flour.
II. Let dough rise for an hour.
III. While the dough is resting, season flank steak with pepper and Chef Meritos Steak Seasoning.
IV. Cook flank steak on high heat until perfect medium rare (Approximately 3-5 minutes).
V. Set steak aside for 10 minutes and thinly slice.
VI. Dice orange bell pepper and sauté in skillet for 3 minutes.
VII. Roll out the dough into desired flatbread shape and base the dough with butter and Italian crushed seasoning.
VIII. Layer with marinara and mozzarella cheese.
IX. Design pizza to your liking.
X. Cook in the oven or Traeger at 450°F for 10-15 minutes.

AVOCADO CREMA
I. Toss 1 avocado, ½ bunch of cilantro, 1 clove of garlic, 3 tablespoons of lime juice, 1 teaspoon of apple cider vinegar, and 8 tablespoons of avocado oil into a blender.
II. Blend for 1 minute, or until desired consistency is achieved.
III. Drizzle over pizza.

FLATBREADS
JAMBALAYA PIZZA

SERVING
1-3 PERSONS

PREP
15 MINUTES

COOK
75 MINUTES

TOTAL
90 MINUTES

FORMULA

INGREDIENTS	AMOUNT
WATER	⅓ CUP
SALT	PINCH
OIL	1 TSP
BUTTER	2 TBSP
DRY YEAST	1 TSP
SUGAR	PINCH
ALL PURPOSE FLOUR	¾ CUP
SHRIMP	¼ LB
ANDOUILLE SAUSAGE	1 LINK
PARSLEY	½ TBSP
RED ONION	TO TASTE
RED PEPPER FLAKES	TO TASTE
SHREDDED PEPPER JACK CHEESE	TO TASTE
MARINARA SAUCE	TO TASTE
MOZZARELLA CHEESE	TO TASTE
CELERY	TO TASTE
CAJUN SEASONING	½ TBSP
GARLIC PEPPER	½ TBSP

PROCESS

I. Thoroughly combine the following dough ingredients: 1/3 cup of warm water, pinch of salt, 1 teaspoon of oil, 1 teaspoon of dry yeast, pinch of sugar, and 3/4 cup of all-purpose flour.
II. Let dough rise for an hour.
III. Season ¼ pound of shrimp with ½ tablespoon of Cajun seasoning, garlic, pepper, and parsley.
IV. Saute the shrimp on each side for 2 minutes on high heat.
V. Saute the Andouille sausage, red onion, and celery for 2 minutes on high heat.
VI. Roll out the dough into desired flatbread shape and base it with melted butter and Italian crushed seasoning.
VII. Layer with marinara, mozzarella, and pepper jack cheese.
VIII. Design pizza to your liking with sausage, shrimp, red onion, and celery.
IX. Cook in the oven or Traeger at 450°F for 10-15 minutes.

SURF

TURF

LOBSTER

LOBSTER BISQUE

SERVING	PREP	COOK	TOTAL
6 PERSONS	12 MINUTES	65 MINUTES	77 MINUTES

FORMULA

INGREDIENTS	AMOUNT		
LOBSTER TAILS	2	BAY LEAVES	2
HEAVY WHIPPING CREAM	1/4 CUP	FRESH THYME	3 SPRIGS
GARLIC	2 CLOVES	CAYENNE PEPPER	1 TBSP
BUTTER	4 CUPS	GARLIC POWDER	1 TBSP
CHARDONNAY	1/2 CUP	SALT	1 TBSP
CHICKEN BROTH	3 CUPS	PEPPER	1 TBSP
FIRE ROASTED ROTEL	10 OZ	OLIVE OIL	¼ CUP
LEMON	1/2	SHALLOT	1
HALF AND HALF	1/2 CUP	FENNEL	1 BUNCH
TOMATO PASTE	2 TBSP	YELLOW ONION	1

PROCESS

LOBSTER- BETTER WITH BUTTER

I. Lobster 1: Extract lobster tail from the shell by cutting down the spine with scissors and using your fingers to guide the meat out of the shell. Finely chop tail
Lobster 2: Extract lobster tail from the shell by cutting down the spine with scissors and using your fingers to guide the meat out of the shell. Leave as is.

II. Season lobster with salt, pepper, garlic powder, and cayenne pepper-- ½ tablespoon of each.

III. Lobster 1: Butter poach chopped tail for 3-5 minutes on high heat.
Lobster 2: Place extracted meat on top of lobster tail and place on high broil until the shell turns opaque (Approximately 5-7 minutes)

BISQUE- WORTH THE WAIT

I. In a skillet, sauté the diced onion and shallot in 1/4 cup of olive oil for 3-5 minutes.

II. Smash 2 garlic cloves with the blade of the knife and extract the shell casing. Add garlic cloves, fennel, and tomato paste into the skillet.

III. Stir the mixture until it turns from a bright to dark red.

IV. Deglaze the skillet by adding chardonnay and scraping all bits from the pan.

V. Note: Don't worry, you will strain the final product for a smooth consistency.
VI. Add chicken stock, Rotel, 2 bay leaves, 2 sprigs of thyme, and 1 tablespoon of cayenne pepper. Cook mixture on a low simmer for 55 minutes.
VII. Filter the bisque base through a sieve into a new pot.
VIII. Stir in ¼ cup of heavy whipping cream, ½ cup of Half and Half, and a squeeze of lemon. Continue to whisk over low heat, and season to taste.

`Pro Tip: Cut your time in the kitchen by using an immersion blender.`

IX. Plate and add the chopped lobster. Garnish with a sprig of thyme.
X. Note: For my extreme lobster lovers, place a whole lobster tail into the bisque for a more fulfilling soup.

LOBSTER
STUFFED LOBSTER

 **SERVING** 1 PERSON

 **PREP** 15 MINUTES

 COOK 45 MINUTES

 **TOTAL** 60 MINUTES

FORMULA

INGREDIENTS	AMOUNT
COOKED SALMON	4 OZ
BREAD CRUMBS	⅓ CUP
SHRIMP	5
PARSLEY	1 BUNCH
CRAB MEAT	¼ CUP
PARMESAN	½ CUP
CHOPPED DILL	½ TBSP
EGG	1
LEMON	1
SALT	1 TBSP
GARLIC POWDER	1 TBSP
PEPPER	1 TBSP
BUTTER	4 TBSP

PROCESS

LOBSTER - STUFF IT!

I. Take the tip of the knife and create a deep slit from the head of the lobster to the tail.

II. Cook salmon: refer to Salmon Filet recipe on page 107.

III. Combine 1 egg, ⅓ cup of bread crumbs, 5 chopped shrimp, 4 oz of chopped cooked salmon, ¼ cup of crab meat, ½ tablespoon of chopped dill, and a handful of chopped parsley in a bowl.

IV. Clean and butter the inside of the lobster, and season with 1 tablespoon of each of the following: salt, garlic powder, and pepper. Add stuffing.

V. Squeeze a lemon atop the lobster and place in the oven at 425°F for 35 minutes.

TRAEGER TREATMENT

I. This ultimate seafood dish deserves the Traeger treatment... I mean come on, we have shrimp, crab, salmon, and lobster all in one! Squeeze a lemon atop stuffed lobster and smoke in Traeger at 425°F for 35 minutes.

SALMON

SALMON TORTELLINI

SERVING — 4-6 PERSONS
PREP — 5 MINUTES
COOK — 20 MINUTES
TOTAL — 25 MINUTES

FORMULA

INGREDIENTS	AMOUNT
5 OZ SALMON FILETS	2
CREAM CHEESE	4 OZ
HEAVY WHIPPING CREAM	½ CUP
TORTELLINI NOODLES	1 LB
PEPPER	1 ½ TBSP
GARLIC POWDER	1 TBSP
ONION POWDER	1 TBSP
CAJUN SEASONING	1½ TBSP
PARSLEY	1 TBSP
MOZZARELLA CHEESE	½ CUP
OLIVE OIL	½ CUP
SALT	½ TBSP
RANCH DRY SEASONING	1 TBSP
GARLIC	2 TBSP

PROCESS

NOODLES- CHEESE-STUFFED TORTELLINI IS THE GO-TO
I. In a pot, bring 4 cups of water to a boil.
II. Add in the tortellini noodles and cook until it rises to the surface.

SALMON- 2 FILETS WILL DO THE TRICK!
I. Season with 1 tablespoon of each of the following: garlic powder, Cajun seasoning, onion powder, pepper, and parsley.
II. Cook each side of salmon with ¼ cup of olive oil on medium-high heat for 2.5 minutes.

ALFREDO- YOU'LL NEVER USE STORE-BOUGHT AGAIN!
I. Add ½ cup of heavy whipping cream into a sauce pan on medium-high heat until it begins to bubble.
II. Don't turn your back too long.. It will crawl out of the pot (I hope you never have to find out what i mean by this).
III. Season with ½ tablespoon of salt and Cajun seasoning, 1 tablespoon of ranch dry seasoning, garlic powder and parsley, and 1 ½ tablespoons of black pepper.
IV. Add 4 ounces of cubed cream cheese and ½ cup of mozzarella cheese. Reduce to a simmer; vigorously stir until Alfredo thickens to a smooth consistency.

Justin Robinson

SALMON

SALMON FILET

SERVING
1 PERSON

PREP
2 MINUTES

COOK
10 MINUTES

TOTAL
12 MINUTES

FORMULA

INGREDIENTS	AMOUNT
5 OZ SALMON FILET	1
WHITE ASPARAGUS	1 BUNCH
LEMON	1
ROMANESCO	1 HEAD
GROUND GINGER	1 TBSP
SALT	1 TBSP
PEPPER	1 TBSP
THYME	1 TBSP
OLIVE OIL	1/4 CUP

PROCESS

SALMON - CATCH OF THE DAY!

I. Season each side of the filet with 1 tablespoon of each of the following: salt, pepper, thyme, and ground ginger.

II. Sear each side of the salmon for approximately 2.5 minutes with ¼ cup of olive oil on medium-high heat.

III. Remove salmon filet and squeeze fresh lemon atop.

SIDES - HEALTHY EATS: A DIVERSE CHOICE!

I. Blanch romanesco while asparagus is cooking.

II. In a pot, bring 3 cups of water to a boil; blanch romanesco for 5 minutes then remove.

III. Sauté white asparagus in the same skillet as salmon for 3-5 minutes to combine flavors.

IV. Season sides with salt and pepper to taste.

Justin Robinson

SURF & TURF

STEAK

STEAK 2 WAYS

SERVING
2 PERSONS

PREP
10 MINUTES

COOK
10 MINUTES

TOTAL
20 MINUTES

FORMULA

INGREDIENTS	AMOUNT
GARLIC POWDER	1 TBSP
DALE'S MARINADE	3 TBSP
STEAKHOUSE SEASONING	1 TBSP
PEPPER	1 TBSP
CANOLA OIL	¼ CUP
THYME	SPRIG
BUTTER	3 TBSP
GARLIC	1 CLOVE
RIBEYE STEAK	10-12 oz

PROCESS

I. Filet ribeye into 2 perfect circles. Mince the remaining trimmings.

II. Soak the steaks and trimmings with 3 tablespoons of Dale's marinade.

III. Season both filets & trimmings with ½ tablespoon of the following on each side: Kinders buttery steakhouse seasoning, pepper, and garlic powder.

IV. Note: Allow marinated steaks to sit for 10 minutes, or overnight for best results.

V. Smoke the round filets on the Traeger at 335°F until internal temperature reaches 125°F: a perfect rare.

VI. Transfer steak filets from the grill to a cast iron skillet on high heat on stove top.

VII. Add 3 tablespoons of butter, a sprig of thyme, and a clove of garlic; base the steak with the aromatics of the butter/garlic/thyme mixture for 2-3 minutes until internal temperature reaches 135°F: a perfect medium rare.

VIII. Cook the remaining minced trimmings in canola oil for 4-5 minutes on high heat. Stir occasionally.

LAMB
RACK OF LAMB

SERVING	PREP	COOK	TOTAL
5-8 PERSONS	7 MINUTES	5 MINUTES	12 MINUTES

FORMULA

INGREDIENTS	AMOUNT
LAMB	1 RACK
POTATOES	4
BUTTER	1 TBSP
OF MILK	1/4 CUP
SALT	1/2 TBSP
PEPPER	1/2 TBSP
MINT	1/2 TBSP
THYME	1/2 TBSP
WATER	4 CUPS
CANOLA OIL	3 TBSP
MILK	¼ CUP

PROCESS

LAMB- RACKS ON RACKS ON RACKS!
I. Cut rack of lamb into single chops.
II. Coat the lamb chops with ½ tablespoon of each of the following: salt, pepper, mint, and thyme.
III. Lightly oil a cast iron skillet.
IV. Cook lamb on each side for 3-5 minutes using medium-high heat for the perfect medium-rare.

POMME PUREÉ - 1 POTATO, 2 POTATO, 3 POTATO, 4!
I. In a pot, bring 4 cups of water to a boil.
II. Chop 4 potatoes and add to boiling water.
III. Cook until water has evaporated or until potatoes are soft to the touch.
IV. Combine potatoes, 1 tablespoon of butter, ¼ cup of milk, and 2 tablespoons of salt in a blender.
V. Add more milk in incrementally if the pureé is too thick.

LAMB

LAMB MEATBALLS

SERVING	**PREP**	**COOK**	**TOTAL**
6 PERSONS	15 MINUTES	18 MINUTES	33 MINUTES

FORMULA

INGREDIENTS	AMOUNT
GROUND LAMB	1 LB
ITALIAN SAUSAGE	1 LB
TOMATOES	2
RED BELL PEPPERS	2
PARSLEY	2 TBSP
MINT	2 TBSP
THYME	2 TBSP
SALT	2 TBSP
PEPPER	2 TBSP
ONION POWDER	2 TBSP
GARLIC	1 CLOVE
SPAGHETTI NOODLES	6 OZ
WATER	3½ CUPS

PROCESS

LAMB- RACKS ON RACKS ON RACKS!

I. Grind 1 pound of lamb in a grinder (or use store bought) to combine with 1 pound of Italian ground sausage.

II. Season with 2 tablespoons of each of the following: mint, thyme, pepper, onion powder, and salt. Mix thoroughly. Form meatballs.

III. In a pot, boil 3 1/2 cups of water. Add noodles and begin preparing romesco sauce by placing red bell peppers and tomatoes under a high broil until skin blisters and slightly char.

IV. Add tomatoes, red bell peppers, and 1 clove of garlic in a blender until sauce is formed. Season with salt and pepper to taste.

V. Sauté meatballs on each side for 2-3 minutes on high heat until desired crust is achieved; then finish off in the oven at 410°F for 15 minutes. Plate and enjoy!

LAMB

LAMB ROAST

SERVING	PREP	COOK	TOTAL
8-12 PERSONS	10 MINUTES	70 MINUTES	80 MINUTES

FORMULA

INGREDIENTS	AMOUNT
CAJUN BUTTER INJECTOR	14 OZ
MINT	6 TBSP
THYME	4 TBSP
PEPPER	4 TBSP
SALT	6 TBSP
ROSEMARY	1 BUNCH

PROCESS

LAMB OF THE LAND!

I. Inject roast 6 or 7 times depending on the size of the lamb leg with Cajun Butter Injector.

II. Season generously with mint, thyme, pepper, and salt to cover all surfaces.

III. Note: The purpose of the injector is to seal the flavor inside the lamb.

IV. Place lamb in the oven at 335°F for approximately 1 hour with a few sprigs of rosemary.

V. As you can see, this is a big piece of meat so you have the option to serve homestyle for your family or make a gourmet sandwich.

SURF & TURF

PORK
CLARENCE CROCKPOT ROAST

SERVING	PREP	COOK	TOTAL
10 PERSONS	10 MINUTES	8-10 HOURS	8-10 HOURS

FORMULA

INGREDIENTS	AMOUNT
GREEN BELL PEPPER	2
CAJUN INJECTOR	1
YELLOW ONION	1
JAR OF AU JUS	12 OZ
DARK BROWN GRAVY	2 PACKS
DARK BROWN GRAVY	1 JAR
BUTTER	1 STICK
BANANA PEPPERS	5
BANANA PEPPER JUICE	¼ CUP
CHUCK ROAST	3 LBS
ONION POWDER	4 TBSP
GARLIC POWDER	4 TBSP
SALT	2 TBSP
PEPPER	2 TBSP
CAJUN SEASONING	2 TBSP
DRY RANCH SEASONING	3 TBSP

PROCESS

MAN THE MEAT

I. Inject roast with Cajun Injector 7 times.
II. Generously season with dry ranch seasoning, onion powder, garlic powder, salt, pepper, and Cajun seasoning.
III. Place a stick of butter at the bottom of the crockpot with ½ sliced onion and 1 sliced bell pepper.
IV. Place roast in crockpot; then, add the remaining sliced bell pepper and ½ sliced onion.
V. Add in 5 banana peppers, ¼ cup of banana pepper juice from jar, 1 jar of Au Jus, 1 jar of brown gravy, and 2 packs of dark brown gravy.
VI. Turn on high heat and cook for 8-10 hours.

PORK
CAJUN PORK CHOP

SERVING	PREP	COOK	TOTAL
1 PERSONS	3 MINUTES	12 MINUTES	15 MINUTES

FORMULA

INGREDIENTS	AMOUNT
BONE-IN PORK CHOPS	1
LIME	1
BUTTER	1 TBSP
ROMA TOMATO	2
RED ONION	½
MANGO	1
CILANTRO	1 BUNCH
CANOLA OIL	4 TBSP
CAJUN SEASONING	½ TBSP
MOJITO LIME SEASONING	½ TBSP
SALT	1 ½ TBSP
PEPPER	1 ½ TBSP
GARLIC POWDER	½ TBSP
ONION POWDER	½ TBSP

PROCESS

PORK CHOP

I. Season pork chop with ½ tablespoon of each of the following: Cajun seasoning, Mojito lime seasoning, salt, pepper, garlic powder, and onion powder.

II. Lightly oil the pan and sear pork chop on each side for 6 minutes.

III. Pro Tip: Visualize a clock. To achieve perfect grilled lines, using a cast iron griddle, turn your chop at 3 o'clock for 3 minutes then 9 o'clock for 3 minutes. Repeat the process on the other side once flipped.

IV. Set aside and add 1 tablespoon of butter and a squeeze of lime while the pork chop rests.

RICE - 2:1 RATIO

I. In a pot, add 1 cup of rice in 2 cups of boiling water.

II. Chop 1 bunch of cilantro and add into rice once water has evaporated, along with 1 tablespoon of salt, pepper, butter, and a squeeze of lime.

SALSA- A TROPICAL PARADISE

I. Dice ½ red onion, 2 Roma tomatoes, 1 mango, and a handful of cilantro.

II. Combine in a bowl and add salt and pepper to taste.

YOUR SPECIAL
NOTES

YOUR SPECIAL
NOTES

YOUR SPECIAL
NOTES

_____
_____
_____
_____
_____
_____
_____
_____
_____
_____
_____
_____
_____
_____
_____
_____
_____

YOUR SPECIAL
NOTES

YOUR SPECIAL
NOTES

YOUR SPECIAL
NOTES

YOUR SPECIAL
NOTES